VISHWAVIDYALAYA
The lost knowledge of INDIA

Anurodh Das

CONTENTS

ACKNOWLEDGEMENTS

I am deeply thankful to the numerous people whose contributions have enriched the pages of this book and deepened my expertise of the historical Indian educational history. Special thanks to Ms. Sahana Singh for her seminal works "Educational Heritage Of Ancient India" and "Revisiting the Educational Heritage of India," which served as priceless resources in deepening my knowledge about the Vishwavidyalayas and the Ancient Indian education system. Her meticulous research and insightful evaluation have illuminated the path for endless scholars and enthusiasts alike.

I am indebted to the scholars, historians, and archaeologists whose groundbreaking research has shed light at the hidden gem stones of our cultural history. Their determination to keep and decoding the beyond has paved the way for a deeper appreciation of the Vishwavidyalayas and their enduring legacy.

Finally, my heartfelt thanks to the readers who embark on this adventure with me. Your interest and thirst for understanding encourage me to retain exploring the wealthy tapestry of human records.

VISHWAVIDYALAYA

In today's time, especially in India, every student has a wish to go to foreign countries such as the United States Of America and the United Kingdom or England for education. This means that nowadays there is a rush to go for abroad studies and become certified by a foreign school or university. But this same rush existed 1000 years ago, not for the Indians, but instead for the Chinese; Tibetan; Greek; Persian students to come to India for their studies and certify themselves from our Ancient Indian learning centres–the Gurukuls and Vishwavidyalayas. The students would walk from distant lands such as China and Tibet to come and learn in India, and most of the students had their main goal to learn more about Buddhism in detail.

The greatest example of this is Xuanzang(602-664 AD) - a Chinese pilgrim and scholar who came to India in 627 AD and stayed here for 16 years till 643 AD. After his stay when he returned back to China, he wrote about his travel accounts and journey during his stay in India named "*Si-Yu-Ki*". He also took back a lot of sacred Buddhist texts from India and translated them from Sanskrit to Chinese. One more pilgrim from China is Fa-Hien, who came to

India 228 years before Xuanzang in 399 AD. You would be shocked to know that when Fa-Hien started his journey to India, he was 60 years old! And he was not alone, he came with his nine other members. He is said to have walked all the way from China across the icy desert and rugged mountain passes.

Thanks to both of them and also Yi-Jing, another Chinese pilgrim and scholar who came to India after Xuanzang in 673 AD. Because of these three people, we can know about Ancient India and Vishwavidyalayas in more detail, such as Nalanda and Takshashila(also spelled Taxila).

<u>ANCIENT UNIVERSITIES AND VARIOUS CENTERS OF LEARNING ACROSS THE INDIAN SUBCONTINENT</u>

<u>Other centres not included in the map:</u>

Manyakheta; Sarvajnapura Agrahara; Salotgi; Udupi Mathha; Kadiyur Agrahara in Karnataka, Ennayiram in Tamil Nadu, Malkapuram in Andhra Pradesh, Nadia in West Bengal, Udaygiri in Odisha.

In Ancient India, the Vishwavidyalayas and other centres of learning were spread across each corner of the Indian subcontinent. The oldest excavated so far is the Takshashila Vishwavidyalaya, which is dated to the 6th century BCE but could be even much older.[1] It was located in the Gandhar region and was also its capital for a time, but today it is located in the Rawalpindi district of the Punjab province in Pakistan.

The others were Nalanda, Odantapuri, Vikramshila, Mithila in Bihar; Pushpagiri, Ratnagiri, Udaygiri in Odisha; Jagaddala, Somapura, Bikrampur in Bangladesh; Varanasi in Uttar Pradesh; Valabhi in Gujarat; Ujjaini in Madhya Pradesh; Sharada Peeth in Kashmir and Kanchipuram in Tamil Nadu; this is only the half of the list though.[1] There is even more to the list! The Archeologists are still finding the remains of other ancient universities or Vishwavidyalayas such as another Vishwavidyalaya's remains were found in Bihar's Telhara village in the Nalanda district in the year 2009. This is the same Telhara Vishwavidyalaya which has also been mentioned by Xuanzang in his travel accounts.

In 2021, Mr. Atul Kumar, a former state archeological director who had earlier led the excavations in Telhara, said that Hiuen Tsang(Xuanzang) called Telhara a seat of learning, where the students would study Mahayana

Buddhism along with other subjects. The sealings found there and the size and shape of the brick, indicate that it was set up around the 1st century AD, even before Nalanda and Vikramshila, which were established centuries later. The layers of Ashes have also been found over the remains during the digging conducted earlier, which means the university would also have been destroyed in the 12th century AD along with Nalanda, Vikramshila, and Odantapuri.[2]

Excavated Ancient Telhara university.   Courtesy: The Indian Express

Today, if a student completes his school education, then he gets multiple options of subjects which he wants to choose and be admitted to a university specialised in that subject, such as FTII(film and television institute of India) and NIFT(National Institute of Fashion and Technology). Just like that, in Ancient India, when a student would complete his basic education and be willing to learn more, he would also get a plethora of institutions depending on the field in which he wanted to specialise such as the Vedas, logic, mathematics, astronomy, philosophy, classical music, etc. [1]

For example, if a student chose astronomy or mathematics, he could move to Ujjaini University or Vishwavidyalaya(Also known as Ujjain), which was very famous for its academic output in mathematics and astronomy. It contained elaborate laboratories and was on the zero meridian longitude of that time. If Imperialistic Europe had not achieved its control on the scientific discourse, then Ujjain, not Greenwich would have been today's Prime Meridian.[1] Ujjaini has produced a lot of mathematics and astronomy experts such as Brahmagupta, who wrote the *Brāhma-sphuṭa-siddhānta*, a theoretical treatise; *Khanda-khādyaka*, a more practical text. But except for authoring these works, he also defined Gravity as *Gurutvākarṣaṇam*. He is also credited with the first clear description of the Quadratic Equation in his theoretical treatise.

In the same treatise, he was the first one to treat zero as a number in its own right, rather than just simply a placeholder digit. He was the first one to establish basic equations with zero such as $0+1=1$; $0-1=1$ and $0 \times 1 = 1$.[3] His works reached the court of Abū Jaʿfar ʿAbd Allāh ibn Muḥammad al-Manṣūr, simply known by his

Laqab–*Al-Manṣ ūr*, in Baghdad and played a significant role in making the Arabs knowing about the Indian mathematics and astronomy.[1]

Another expert from Ujjaini was Bhaskara II, also known as Bhaskaracharya, who was the head of the astronomical observatory at Ujjaini and wrote the famous *Siddhānta Shiromani* and Līlāvatī. He is considered to be the first mathematician to write a work with full and systematic use of the decimal number system, and he is also considered the founder of Differential Calculus, who applied it centuries before Newton and Leibniz.[1]

However, just like this, if a student was willing to learn classical music, he could move to Varanasi and learn from the maestros of the city's ancient College of Music. And on the way, if he found a friend keen on studying another subject, they both could travel together.[1] By the way, travelling was a risky activity to do in those days, since there were more jungles filled with predators. Because of this, many parents would fear for their children, and when a student would come back to his home after studying for 5 to 10 years, their parents would celebrate the moment![1]

At the end of the theoretical education in the Vishwavidyalayas, extensive foreign travel was required, which was insisted especially for the students from rich families to learn the hardship of travelling and enduring heat and cold.[7]

So as you can see, the importance of education was realised in India in the early times, and the utmost emphasis was laid upon the obtainment of education.[4] The educational institutes were spread across all over India in their different forms. If we talk about their complex form, it was none other than the Vishwavidyalayas. And if we talk about their simplest form, it was the Gurukuls, or in other words, the gathering of one or more students in the house of the Guru or teacher.[4] The term "Gurukul" itself is a combination of the Sanskrit words *"Guru"*(Teacher) and *"Kula"*(home) and the term means "Home of the Guru". Nowadays, the image of Gurukuls in the minds of the people is like this— a group of students in Brahmanical attire sitting on the ground and the teacher, also in Brahmanical attire, sitting under a tree(most commonly a Banyan tree) in a forest; which is right by the way, but not all the Gurukuls were in forests though, some were located in the huts of the villages and some in the houses of the towns. This is because the Gurus usually were householders of their families. However, most of the time secluded locations were preferred.[1]

Regarding both the Gurukuls and Vishwavidyalayas, most people think that education was free of cost. This is correct in some cases, but most of the time, the student had to give a token gift or *Guru-Dakshina* to his Guru. While there were also students from poor families who could not afford to give the Dakshina, they had to do menial tasks instead of this. While the students from rich families, or usually rich Brahmins, gave huge honorarium as Guru-Dakshina.[4] These Guru-Dakshinas were usually taken at the end of a student's course, but in some cases, it was taken as an advance payment before the beginning of the course. But if a student from a poor family was not able to afford it, he had to give it at the end of the course.

Besides the Gurukuls and Vishwavidyalayas, there were also temple universities. Nowadays we see temples only as a place of worship, but in ancient times, the temples were also a huge hub of learning, where the Shishyas or students would come to learn with their Gurus inside the temple premises. One such example is the Azhagiya Narasimma Perumal temple of Ennayiram in Tamil Nadu, which was also a Vedic college during the Chola period, and had hostels and hospitals attached to it.

Azhaga Narasimma Perumal temple in Ennayiram, Tamil Nadu in present day.

But the list has not yet ended, there was another temple university at Thiruvananthapuram in Kerala named Kanthalloor Shala, also known as *Sarva Chattanamadam*. This university was supported by the Cholas and was also called "the Nalanda of South India" because of the variety of subjects taught there such as the Vedas, grammar, philosophy, logic, science, mathematics, martial arts, music, and painting which are mentioned in *Kuvalayamala*, a Prakrit work written by *Uddyotana Sūri,* an Eighth Century CE Jain monk from Rajasthan.[1] By the way, The temple was previously located at Vizhinjam but was relocated to Thiruvananthapuram after a Chola attack.

So, now let's move from South India to the very north state of India, which is Kashmir. Nowadays it is difficult to imagine a renowned temple university in POK, Pakistan-occupied Kashmir, but there was a temple university in that region that existed in the pre-Islamic period, called Sharada Peeth. This temple university was named after Saraswati, the goddess of learning, who is also known as Sharada.[1] It played a significant role in spreading and popularising of the Sharada script in North India, which was named after itself and Kashmir got its new nickname *"Sharada Desh"* which means the country of Sharada.

There are various associated figures with it, such as Swami Ramanuja, the famous *Vaishnava* saint, in the 11th century CE travelled from Srirangam at Tiruchirappalli in Tamil Nadu to Sharada Peeth to refer to the Brahma Sutras, before commencing his commentary work on the Brahma Sutras named *Sri Bhasya*.[1] Another major figure is Thonmi Sambhota, the inventor of the Tibetan script, who was first sent to Kashmir on a mission to procure an alphabet for the Tibetan language, where he learnt various scripts and grammar treatises from learned *Pandits*, after which he devised the Tibetan script, largely based on the Sharada alphabet. Rinchen Zangpo, a translator of Sanskrit texts into Tibetan is said to have studied there. Adi Shankaracharya is said to have gained the title of *Jagadguru* after answering the questions of the scholars of Sharada Peeth and is also said to have opened its south door.[1]

The ruins of Sharada Peeth   Photo by Umar Jaimshaid

Till now, as we have seen, the Ancient Indians attached so much value to the learning, and so it should not be a surprise that there was also a ceremony to mark the Graduation of students. Yes! There was a rite of passage for marking the graduation of students in ancient India called Samāvartana or *Snāna*. In the august presence of students, teachers, and guests, the graduating student would offer his Guru-Dakshina and then the Guru would recite the Snataka-Dharma from the *Taittiriya Upanishad*. After which, the ceremony would be followed by a Homa or fire ritual and Snana or ceremonial bath. After the whole ceremony, the student was granted permission by his Guru to return home. This ceremony would mark the end of a student's formal education and *Brahmacharya* period, and also the starting of *Grihasthashram*, meaning a married life. However, the students had the option to choose either to marry or continue to study and teach. Besides this, the student who had completed this rite of passage was considered a Vidya-Snataka, meaning showered with learning or bathed in knowledge, and was also symbolised as one who had crossed the ocean of learning. By the way, Samavartana translates to "Now you are equal to me(Guru)" or "Now you will behave like me(Guru)".

Okay!, so now, since you all have understood the concept of Vishwavidyalaya(Actually more than that) we can continue to the next chapters to learn more in detail about the four major universities of Ancient India – Takshashila, Nalanda, Odantapuri and Vikramshila.

TAKSHASHILA

Ruins of Takshashila in Rawalpindi, Pakistan   Photo by Shasha Isachenko

INTRODUCTION

Takshashila, referred to as Taxila by the Greeks, is the oldest university or Vishwavidyalaya ever founde d, which dates to the 6th century BCE or even further to 1000 BCE. In the Jātaka tales, it is mentioned about Takshashila as a centre of great learning. It has also been mentioned in both *Ramayana* and *Mahabharata*, which clearly shows its significance! In *Ramayana*, it is mentioned that the city was founded by *Bhagwan Rama's* younger brother *Bharata*, who named the city after his son *Taksha*, who was the first ruler of Takshashila. He is also said to have founded the city of Pushkalavati, which was named after his second son *Puskala*, who was also the first ruler of the city. In *Mahabharata*, it is mentioned that *Parikshit*, the grandson of *Arjuna* and heir to the *Kuru* kingdom, ruled Takshashila. It is also believed that *Mahabharata* was first recited at Takshashila by Vaisampayana, a famous disciple of Guru Vyasa.[1]   It is now located in the Rawalpindi district of the Province of Punjab in Pakistan, but earlier it used to be the capital of the Gandhara kingdom which also included the cities of Pushkalavati and Purushapura(Peshawar).

But since Takshashila had seen several annexes, it had gotten the chance to get exposure to the different cultures of the world. And let me remind you, The Gandhara region where Takshashila was located had been a part of the invasion of the Achaemenid empire or Alexander's invasion. Apart from this, it had also been annexed by the Seleucid Empire, the Indo-Greek Empire of Bactria, the Indo-Scythian Empire, and the Indo-Parthian Empire. The Greek historians accompanying Alexander described Takshashila as "wealthy, prosperous, and well-governed". This Vishwavidyalaya was visited by several travellers such as Megasthenes, who came as an ambassador at the court of King Chandragupta Maurya, and also Fa-hien in 405 AD, who has mentioned both the university and city in his travel accounts. It was also visited by Xuanzang, but he only found the ruins of the university, since it was destroyed around 455 AD.[1] According to the early Christian legend, Thomas the Apostle visited Takshashila, who preached at the court of King Gondophares, and this might be the reason behind why there is a church named "St. Thomas The Apostle Catholic Church" at Takshashila.

EDUCATION AND SCHOLARS

Takshashila has made great contributions to the Sanskrit language as well as to world culture. It is said that Takshashila had students from huge and famous parts of the world at that time, such as Greece, China, Babylon and Syria.[5] The students also came from Magadha, Kosala and Kashi. A student's minimum age at the time of admission was approximately 16 years. It is said that Takshashila had more than 10,000 students! The Jātaka tales, written around the 5th century AD in Sri Lanka, frequently mention Takshashila. Just like in one of those mentions, we get to know that the students who went to Takshashila for higher education, were taught the Vedas. Apart from this, there were 18 Sippas(arts) that were taught there, which included scientific and technical education. Takshashila also had special schools that taught medicine, law, and military sciences.[1] Also, since there was a huge Greek influence in the Gandhara region, the Vishwavidyalaya also taught Greek grammar and linguistics, and because of this, there were several scholars who became fluent in Greek. The curriculum of Takshashila consisted of more than 60 elective courses which included philosophy, law, statecraft, defence, warfare strategies, grammar, the 18 Sippas or arts, mathematics, astronomy, astrology, plants & herbs, medicine(Ayurveda, Ayurvedic acupuncture, etc.), economics, politics, and surgery.[4] Some of these courses, such as medicine, were taught up to 7 years before the Samavartana or Graduation.

Jivaka, a royal physician of King Bimbisara and Ajatashatru, and even Buddha, was a Takshashila alumnus in medicine who studied here for 7 long years. Just like him, Takshashila had produced some very well-known and great scholars such as Chanakya! who was also an alumnus of Takshashila, whose famous *Arthashastra* is believed to be composed at Takshashila itself! and it is also said that Chanakya took King Chandragupta Maurya to Takshashila where he mentored him. Another famous scholar was Panini, who had a major role in unravelling the mysteries of Sanskrit Grammar. He wrote the famous *Aṣ ṭ ādhyāyī* which is a grammar that describes the Sanskrit language, or basically it is the grammar of Sanskrit which contains nearly *4000 sūtras*. Charaka, who has given crucial contributions to Ayurveda and also wrote the famous *Charaka Samhita*, was also an alumni of the Vishwavidyalaya. Even Vishnu Sharma, the author of the famous *Panchatantra* is also believed to have studied at Takshashila.[1]

PRACTICAL TRAINING

The most major part of the education of Takshashila was its Practical training, which was required in every field of study. For example, in the practical course of medicine, a thorough knowledge of medicinal plants was required.[1] This is perfectly shown in the story by Jivaka that when he completed his study of medical science from Takshashila after 7 years, his Guru took a device to test his knowledge. "Take this spade" he said, "And seek round about Takshashila a *yojana* on every side, and whatever plant you see is not medicinal bring it to me". So according to the Guru, Jivaka walked around Takshashila and every side but he wasn't able to find any plant which is not medicinal. When he came back to his Guru and said this to him, he was satisfied with his pupil's learning and allowed him to go home.[4] Apart from this, Jivaka is also cited to perform successful surgeries on patients as a part of his practical demonstration. However, as I said earlier that at the end of the theoretical education in the Vishwavidyalayas, and even Takshashila, extensive foreign travel was required, which was insisted especially for the students from rich families to learn the hardship of travelling and enduring heat and cold. There are several stories in the Jātaka tales about the students from Takshashila, travelling after completing their education.[7]

STUDENT LIFE

The student life at Takshashila was characterised by strict rules, which is evident from the facts that the students were required to follow a simple lifestyle and eat similar food, and they were also not allowed to possess money while studying there. A student was not even allowed to go to a river for a bath, without the company of a Guru. The life of the students was also hard in different ways, such as their standing duty was to gather firewood in the forests.[7] With this, the door to Takshashila was closed for incompetent students to maintain the reputation of the Vishwavidyalaya. Qualities like self-discipline, honesty, and modesty were necessary for a student to obtain admission. The admission to Takshashila was not only limited to the students belonging to the elite class, some evidence mentions the sons of kings, nobles, merchants, tailors, and even fishermen getting education at Takshashila. The only class who were not eligible to get admission in the Vishwavidyalaya was Chandala. There is an instance when two Chandalas disguised as Brahmins came to Takshashila and got education in law but were soon banished after their guise was detected in a dinner. However, there was no formal examination system, this was because the Gurus used the mode of teaching which was analytical and meticulous, and they considered the examinations unnecessary. Interestingly, unlike today's education system, there were no degrees, certificates, or diplomas awarded to students upon the completion of their studies from Takshashila.[6]

TEACHER LIFE

The teachers or Gurus of Takshashila were highly respected by their students or Shisyas. They had a lot of autonomy, including the ability to choose a student and design their syllabi. Since managing a school of more than 500 pupils was not an easy job for an individual teacher, that is why, they took help from the assistant masters, who were none other than the advanced or senior students, who assisted their Gurus in teaching. Because of this association with teaching, these senior pupils would soon become fit to be teachers. They trusted each other, which would strengthen their bond even closer. This can be understood by an instance, when a Guru from Takshashila was going to Kashi(Varanasi) on some mission, he appointed his chief student to take charge of his school during his absence. Apart from this, since Takshashila had a number of sittings every day, the Gurus would teach by shifts in both day and night. The schedules of the Gurus were not rigid, instead, they were flexible and catered to the student's schedules. And as I mentioned on pg. 9, that students from poor families who were not able to afford the *Guru-Dakshina* would do menial tasks in lieu. These students would perform these tasks during the daytime, and because of this, they had the time to study only during the night time. Besides this, if we talk about the bond between a Guru and his Shishya, it would be more like a father and son.[7]

DESTRUCTION

Now after all the details of Takshashila, let us discuss how this huge Vishwavidyalaya was destroyed? and who was behind it? Well, the answer to both these questions can be a mystery. Now I know that most of the people(who have some knowledge about the deeper history) think that it was the White Huns who destroyed Takshashila. But this is just a theory because nobody can guarantee that only the Huns were behind the destruction and decline of Takshashila. As I mentioned on pg. 16, by the time Xuanzang visited Takshashila it had already been ruined by the 7th century CE, and he was also the first person to mention the destruction of Takshashila. But, he didn't directly mention that the Huns were the ones behind this destruction. Besides this, no direct Indian accounts mention the Huns behind this destruction. But then also, why do most people believe that the Huns destroyed Takshashila even after a lack of explicit accounts? This is because some archeological evidence at Takshashila suggests the period of disruption and abandonment at Takshashila around the 5th century AD, which is the same time when the Huns were known to sweep central Asia. Apart from any man-made destruction, the cause behind it could also be natural destruction and disaster or internal strife. However, whatever is the reason behind it, the destruction was so massive that neither Takshashila Vishwavidyalaya nor Takshashila city was able to recover from this destruction, thus creating an end of the world's first-ever educational institute and its education, Buddhist monasteries and Stupas in the region.

NALANDA

Ruins of Nalanda Vishwavidyalaya — Source: Wikipedia

INTRODUCTION

After Takshashila, the next institute which came into existence was none other than Nalanda Vishwavidyalaya(also known as Nalanda Mahavihara) and as time passed, this University became a huge centre of learning as well as Mahayana Buddhism. It was the world's first-ever residential university which attracted students from all over Asia, and even Gulf countries! Till now, the most detailed description of an ancient university we have, is Nalanda! Once again, thanks to the writings of Xuanzang and Yi-Jing. Nalanda was established in the Gupta Period around the 5th Century AD, particularly in 427 AD during the rule of King Kumaragupta, and was patronised by several emperors. The site on which Nalanda was established, used to be a village or suburb called *Nalo*, which was visited by Gautam Buddha and also Fa-Hien. It was located near the city Rajagriha(Today's Rajgir) which was 60 kilometres away from the Southeast of Pataliputra(today's Patna). The word "Nalanda" is a combination of Sanskrit words "Na", "Alam" and "Daa" which means "no stopping of the gift of knowledge" or "insatiable in giving" which is, in fact, one of the names of Buddha. But the name may also come from the words "Nalam" and "Da" which means "Giver of knowledge".

INFRASTRUCTURE

One of the most unique factors of the Nalanda Vishwavidyalaya was its over-the-top infrastructure, which is hugely praised and mentioned by Xuanzang and Yi-Jing. Nalanda in its prime time, had the world's largest infrastructure for Buddhist studies between the 6th century and 12th century AD. There are references that Nalanda was spread over an area of 16 sq. kilometres, of which only an area of 1 sq. kilometre has been excavated.[11] The university was enveloped by a lofty gate and high walls, with all the buildings arranged in a linear alignment from North to South. It contained numerous lecture halls and residential quarters for both the Gurus and Shisyas. It also had laboratories and Observatories. Yi-Jing mentions in his writings that there were 300 apartments in the monastery. But besides all of these, the most stunning was its nine-storeyed library which was called Dharma Gunj(meaning Treasury of Truth) and was divided into three buildings named Ratnasagar, Ratnaranjak, and the Ratnodadhi. Out of them, the Ratnodadhi housed Nalanda's most sacred manuscripts. The overall library housed millions of manuscripts on a variety of subjects, including religion, philosophy, astronomy, and medicine. According to Xuanzang, the university opened with a big main hall which was separated from eight other halls. He also mentions that from the upper towers of these halls, one could see the wind and clouds producing new forms, and from the overhang from the roof, splendid sunsets and moonlit glories could be seen.[1]

PATRONAGE

Throughout an unbroken period of 800 years, Nalanda attracted students from distant lands as well as received patronage from various local and foreign rulers.[8] It was also supported by numerous Indian and Javanese patrons(both Buddhists and Non-Buddhists). Nalanda mainly flourished under the patronage of the Gupta rulers in the 5th and 6th centuries, and in the 7th century, it received patronage from King Harsha of Kannauj, and then from the 8th to 12th century the Pala rulers patronised Nalanda. These rulers made massive developments and constructions of impressive buildings that were majestic in their size with richly adorned towers, which looked like hilltops in Nalanda.[1] Xuanzang in his accounts mentions his great relationship with King Harsha who also invited him to his court for a debate. In that debate, Xuanzang defeated all his opponents, which further impressed King Harsha and their bond grew stronger. In his writings, he praises the deeds of King Harsha.[13] Through the writings of Xuanzang and the inscriptions found in Nalanda, we get to know that Emperor Harshvardhan was one of the most celebrated patrons of Nalanda who built temples, monasteries, and Viharas here.[9] However, the patronage of Nalanda was not limited to only local kings, there is evidence that kings from foreign lands too donated Nalanda for the building of structures in the Nalanda complex. There is archaeological evidence of King Shailendra of Indonesia who built a structure within the campus.[10] Besides building structures, the kings also supplied all the necessary materials for the Gurus and Shisyas. The revenue of about 100 villages was remitted for this purpose, and about 200 householders of these villages supplied in turn the daily needs of the inmates. Yi-Jing mentions in his writings, that since the students were being abundantly supplied, they weren't required to ask for the four basic needs; clothes, food, bedding, and medicine.[4]

EDUCATION AND CURRICULUM

A wide range of subjects were taught in Nalanda, which included both sacred and secular, philosophical and practical, sciences and arts which according to Xuanzang was the most complete education available at that time.[1] As per ASI records, the subjects taught in Nalanda included Theology, grammar, logic, astronomy, metaphysics, medicine, and philosophy.[11] But besides Theology and Philosophy, frequent debates and discussions took place at Nalanda which were necessary for competence in Logic. A student at the Vishwavidyalaya had to be well-versed in the systems of logic associated with different schools of thought of the time. Other subjects that were taught in Nalanda include city planning, Law, and Astronomy.[14] Xuanzang himself studied several subjects including Yoga Shastra under Silabhadra, the highest authority of that time. He also studied Nyay, Hetuvidya, Shabdavidya, and the Sanskrit grammar of Panini.[1] The students at Nalanda were also taught the Vedas, Medicine, and Sankhya Philosophy.[4] More than 100 lectures were held at Nalanda in a single day! and as per Yi-Jing, the students did not want to miss even a minute of these lectures.[12] According to Tibetan traditions, the four *Grub-Mtha* or doxographies: *Sarvastivada Vaibhashika*; *Sarvastivada Sautrantika*; *Madhyamaka*, the Mahayana philosophy of Nagarjuna; *Chittamatra*, the Mahayana philosophy of Asanga and Vasubandhu, were taught at Nalanda.[15] In the 7th century AD, Xuanzang recorded the number of teachers at Nalanda being around 1510. Of these, about 1000 teachers were able to explain 20 collections of Sutras and Shastras; 500 teachers were able to explain 30 collections; and only 10 teachers were able to explain 50 collections. At that time, only Shilabhadra had studied all the major collections of sutras and shastras available at Nalanda. And Xuanzang being a pupil of Silabhadra, was among the few who were able to explain 50 collections or more.[7]

ENTRANCE EXAMINATION

Getting admission to a World-Class university like Nalanda was as tough as getting admission in today's Harvard and Oxford. According to the writings of Xuanzang, Nalanda had a tough entrance examination. Only about 20% of the students who applied got through the examination and only they had the right to enter Nalanda. The test was even tougher for foreign students since they had to be deeply versed in old and modern learning.[1]   The exam was conducted by the gatekeepers of Nalanda, and they rejected those who did not pass their rigid examination. Xuanzang mentions that the gatekeepers of Nalanda were way more intelligent than him. The examinations were verbal, probably discussions or debates.[16] But, there was also a separate department for secondary education which took in young students, for whom the entrance examinations were not conducted.[7]

PRACTICES FOLLOWED IN NALANDA

First of all, one of the most common practices followed by the ascetics in Nalanda was *Bhiksha*, which means the practice of requesting food from households, which is wrongfully regarded as begging nowadays. But in ancient times, it was regarded as a respectable activity.[7][1] The unique teaching practices followed by the Gurus were among the reasons for the popularity of Nalanda. Those practices included debate, discussion, and interaction between the students and teachers. The students were encouraged to ask questions and challenge their teachers' views. The university expected the students to contribute to the society in some way, such as through research, invention, or achievement in a particular field.[17]

SCHOLARS OF NALANDA

The list of the scholars of Nalanda is very long! That's why this section is also going to be a bit longer. So first, let's start with the seventeen Pandits of Nalanda, which refers to the group of seventeen of the most important and influential Mahayana Buddhist masters from India who are associated with Nalanda. Even the Dalai Lama frequently refers to himself as a follower of the lineage of the seventeen Nalanda masters today. But this list of seventeen is also divided into the six ornaments; two excellent or supreme ones; and nine additional Buddhist masters. So now let's see the six ornaments, where the first is Nagarjuna, who was the founder of the middle way(*Madhyamaka*) school of Buddhist philosophy. His work *Mūlamadhyamakakārikā* is the most important text on the *Madhyamaka* philosophy of *Śūnyatā* or

Emptiness. The second ornament is Aryadeva, who was the disciple of Nagarjuna and a *Madhyamaka* philosopher. His writings, *Catuḥ śataka*; **Śataka*; *Dvādaśamukhaśāstra*, are the most important sources of Madhyamaka in East Asian Buddhism. After them are Asanga and his half-brother Vasubandhu. The two were the founders of the *Yogachara* school of Buddhism, also known as the *Yogācāra* school of Buddhism, which is a major school of Mahayana Buddhism, and also serves as an influential tradition in Buddhist philosophy and psychology.[19][18]

After them, the additional two ornaments are Dignaga and Dharmakirti. Dignaga created the first system of *Pramana*(Buddhist logic and epistemology), and he is also one of the Buddhist founders of the *hetu vidyā*. While Dharmakirti is regarded as a grand disciple of Dignaga his work *Pramāṇ avārttika* was most influential in India and Tibet as a central text on *Pramana*.[21]

Now coming forward to the two excellent or supreme ones, it refers to the two great *Vinaya*(ethical discipline) masters, Gunaprabha and Shakyaprabha. Gunaprabha was a disciple of Vasubandhu and is famous for his treatise, the *Vinaya Sutra*. On the other hand, Shakyaprabha was a disciple of Shantarakshita(one of the nine additionals) and is associated with the *Mulasarvastivada-Vinaya* line.

Now let's move on to the nine additional Buddhist masters. Buddhapalita, one of the great commentators on Nagarjuna's *Madhyamaka* thought. Chandrakirti, a philosopher of the *Madhyamaka* school of Nagarjuna. Shantarakshita, a philosopher of the *Madhyamaka* school and the founder of the Sam-Ye monastery, the first-ever Buddhist monastery in Tibet. Kamalashila, a disciple of Shantarakshita is considered one of the most important *Madhyamaka* authors of late Indian Buddhism. Haribhadra, a disciple of Shantarakshita and one of the founding monks of Vikramshila. Arya Vimuktisena, a commentator on Asanga's *Abhisamayalankara*. Shantideva is an adherent of the *Mādhyamaka* philosophy of Nāgārjuna. Now the final master among the seventeen was Atisha, one of the major figures in the spread of 11th-century Mahayana and Vajrayana Buddhism in Asia and inspired Buddhist thought from Tibet to Sumatra.[20][19][18]

But besides the seventeen, there were also several great scholars and teachers from Nalanda, such as King Dharmapala, the son and successor of Gopala(the founder of the Pala dynasty) studied at Nalanda. Then comes King Harshavardhana, who was also a student at Nalanda. Now if we talk about the teachers, the first on the list is Aryabhata, the great Indian mathematician and astronomer behind the establishment of the number zero as a digit in the world. After him comes Shilabhadra and Chandragomin.[22]

DECLINE AND DESTRUCTION: THE ULTIMATE TRAGEDY OF NALANDA AND BUDDHISM

In the 5th century AD, around the time when Nalanda was a newly established University, the Huns under Mihirakula attacked Nalanda. This was the first time Nalanda witnessed an attack. However, the university was restored on a more massive scale, which started attracting students from distant lands. But in the 8th century, Nalanda once again witnessed an attack by the Gauda king of Bengal. While the Huns came to plunder, the exact reason for the attack by the Gaudas can't be concluded whether it was for the growing antagonism between their Shaivite Hindu Sect and the Buddhists at that time. But this time also, the university was restored by King Harsha.[17] And let me remind you, that the 8th century was the time when the Bhakti movement started to grow. By the 12th century, the Bhakti movement had come to North India and saw great growth here.[25] It was also the time when the Pala Dynasty saw its decline after the Hindu Sena Dynasty came into power.[26] With the decline of the Pala Dynasty and the growth of the Bhakti movement, Buddhism also started to decline. As expected, with the decline of Buddhism, Nalanda also lost its prime. The attack by Bakhtiyar Khilji, the general of the army of the Mamluk Dynasty, in the 12th century, put a complete end to Nalanda. He destroyed the whole Vishwavidyalaya, and most importantly the Dharma Gunj, the library of Nalanda. He killed and burnt alive several monks. The few monks who survived the attack flew to Tibet and China.[24][23] Archaeologist H.D Sankalia in his book, "The University of Nalanda", has mentioned the reason behind the invasions in Nalanda, that *"the fortress-like appearance of the campus and stories of its wealth were reasons enough for invaders to deem the university a lucrative spot for an attack"*[24] Now this is not a genocide to ignore, but a genocide that completely changed the destiny of India. And let me tell you, Khilji destroyed not only Nalanda but also Odantapuri and Vikramshila. Unfortunately, because of this genocide, today we are not able to know what precious treasure of knowledge was kept in the Dharma Gunj of Nalanda. Just like Takshashila, we lost another gem of education.

ODANTAPURI

FOUNDATION

In the 8th century CE, with the fall of Shashanka's dynasty, Gopala ascended the throne and established the Pala Dynasty.[29] The ruling period of the Palas is also called the Golden Era in the history of Bengal. They were great patrons of Mahayana Buddhism and played a significant role in spreading Buddhism across the Indian subcontinent. They also made significant contributions to art, literature and architecture. With this, they hugely supported and funded Nalanda University, and also built many Buddhist Mahaviharas across Magadha and Bengal. Among them was the Odantapuri Mahavira or University, which was the second oldest Mahavira after Nalanda.[30] But who exactly founded Odantapuri, can be a question of debate. According to Bu-ston, a 14th-century Tibetan Buddhist leader, Odantapuri was built by Gopala's son and successor Dharmapala, while according to Taranatha, a Lama of the Jonang school of Tibetan Buddhism, it was founded by Devapala, the son and successor of Dharmapala, and also the most powerful ruler of the Pala dynasty. But it is hugely believed that Odantapuri was founded by Gopala, who built it in the 8th century CE after he ascended the throne.[27] Odantapuri was a part of the network of five Mahaviras in Eastern India, the others were Nalanda, Vikramshila, Somapura and Jagaddala. Except Nalanda, all the other Mahaviras were founded by the Palas. During the Pala period, Vikramshila and Odantapuri became the leading monasteries and received more state funding and patronage under the Pala kings than Nalanda, which resulted in Nalanda struggling in the 11th century CE.[28] From the inscriptional evidences, we also get to know that Odantapuri was also getting support from the local Buddhist kings such as the Pitipathis of Bodh Gaya.[31]

TIBETAN HISTORY AND RECORDS

According to Tibetan records, Odantapuri was located at Hiranya Prabhat Parvat and by the bank of the river Panchanan. Currently, Bihar Sharif is believed to be the location where Odantapuri existed.[36] However, Odantapuri became a model and inspiration for Tibetan Buddhists. According to Tibetan sources, the Sam-Ye(Bsam-Yas) monastery was modelled upon it and several Tibetan scholars studied there.[35] According to Tibetan records, there were approximately 12,000 students and 160 professors at Odantapuri from all over

Asia and beyond. According to Taranatha, King Mahapala who he claims to be the son of Mahipala, the eleventh ruler of the Pala dynasty, supported 500 Sravakasangha bhikshus at Odantapuri. As a supplementary building to it, he built a monastery called Uruvasa, where he supported 500 Sendha-Pa or Sendhava Sravaka, the Tibetan reference for a Sravakayana Buddhist school.[34][33]   In the Tibetan history of the Kalachakra Tantra by Jamyang Amnye Zhab Ngawang Kunga Sonam, the 27th Sakya Trizin, it is mentioned that Odantapuri was administered by the Sendhapas.[36]   However, according to Peter Skilling, an author and honorary associate of the Department of Indian Sub-Continental Studies, the Sendhapa Sravakas could have been Sammatiyas since the probable derivation of it is from the Sanskrit Saindhava or 'Residents of Sindh' where the Sammatiyas were the predominant school. But Taranatha links the Sendhapa monks at the Mahabodhi temple at Bodhgaya to the "Singha Island " which includes Sri Lanka and other places.[36]

LEGENDS

There are various legends attached to the establishment of Odantapuri. According to Taranatha, Odantapuri was built using gold which was obtained in a mystical process. He mentioned that a Tantrik or Tirthika Yogi called Narada, who had miraculous and magical powers, needed someone even stronger, brave, and a truthful companion in all branches of knowledge and craft to help him assist in a ritual with a corpse or Shava Sadhana. However, he was not able to find anyone who meets the criteria, except a Buddhist Upasaka, a Sanskrit term used for masculine and also mainly used in Buddhism who are not monks, nuns, or novice monastics in a Buddhist order, and who undertake certain vows. The Upasaka did not want to be the assistant to a Tantrik, but Narada convinced him by promising him a lot of wealth which could be used by the upasaka to spread his religion.

They performed the ritual and as it was reaching fulfilment, Narada said that when the cadaver sticks its lingo out, the upasaka must catch it. He told him that if he catches it in the first pass, he'll attain supreme success(*maha- siddhi*), if he does it in the alternate pass, he'll gain intermediate success, and if he catches it in the third pass, he'll get small success. Still, if he fails to catch it indeed after the third time, the vetala (cadaver) will devour them both and also clear the whole world. After failing to catch the lingo doubly, the upasaka sat with his own mouth near the cadaver's, and caught its lingo with his teeth. But the cadaver turned into gold. When the upasaka held the brand he began to fly in the sky. He flew to the top of Sumeru and circled it along with the four dvipas and their upa-dvipas. When he returned he gave the brand to Narada, who let him have the gold but advised him not to spend it for immoral purposes.

Narada, also flew to heaven, and the upasaka who came to be known as Unna Upasaka erected the colossal tabernacle of Odantapuri using the gold. The tradesmen and artists who worked on the structure were paid with that gold, and it was also used for conservation of 500 bhikshus and 500 upasakas. The gold could not be used by anyone after Unna's death, because he buried the gold under the earth, soliciting that it might profit all living beings in future. Also he handed over the Odantapuri house to king Devapala. Sumpa Khan-Po Yece Pal Jor, a 16th-century author who wrote Pag Sam Jon Zang, which is about the history of Buddhism's rise, progress, and decline, mentioned that Otanta in Otantapuri(Odantapuri) meant "Soaring on high". This might come from the Sanskrit words Uddayana and Uddyanta, meaning "Going up or flying". According to the legend, the temple was called so because Unna had flown over Sumeru and seen the mountain along with its four dvipas, and hence Odantapuri in its model.[38]

In the "Bu ston chos 'byung" or "The history of Buddhism in India and Tibet" which is a historical work written by Bu-ston, he tells the story of Dharmapala's birth and how he built the monastery of Odantapuri. King Gopala's queen and wife, Dedda Devi, also the daughter of a king of the Bhadra dynasty, had no power over Gopala. So to gain power over him, she asked a Brahmin for a magical potion to influence him. Then the Brahmin brought an enchanted drug from the Himalayas and gave it to the queen's maidservant. But while crossing a bridge, the maidservant fell and the drug was carried away by the stream to the ocean, where it was seized and swallowed by the king of Nagas, who ruled the ocean. Because of the drug, he became subject to the queen's power and united with her. After that, they had a son named Dharmapala. But during the religious ceremonies for the child, the head of a serpent haughtily rose which enraged the king. He decided to cut it off, but then a ring was shown to him, in which he beheld the characters of the Nagas. He then continued to worship and devoted his life to the child's education. When Dharmapala grew up, he wanted to build a temple more magnificent than others. So he consulted soothsayers, who told him that it was necessary to make a wick out of cotton belonging to Ascetics and Brahmins, get oil from the houses of kings and merchants, obtain an oil burner from a place of penance, and burn the lamp using those and place it before the tutelary deity. If the king prayed, the serpent of Dharmapala would throw the lamp away and the temple must be built where the lamp falls. The lamp was lit, but suddenly a raven appeared and threw the lamp into a lake. This made Dharmapala distressed, but that night, the king of Nagas came to him and said -- "I am your father, and I will cause this lake to dry up. You shall build your temple in the place of it. To bring this out, you must perform sacrifices for seven weeks." This was done accordingly. On the 21st day, the lake dried up and in its place, the Odantapuri was built.[38][39]

EDUCATION AND ALUMNI

Just like Nalanda, Odantapuri also had a huge library which was a three-story structure with courtyards and terracotta decorations that contained millions of Buddhist and Brahminical books. The library was loftier than Nalanda and Vajrasana(Bodh Gaya). Besides this, various subjects were taught there such as Theology, Grammar, Philosophy, Logic, and Metaphysics. Its monks and scholars were so prolific that with their literary output, the script of *Bhaiksuki* evolved here, which became a standard script in Northern India for writing Buddhist texts such as *Abhidharmasamuccayakārikā* and *Maṇ icūḍ ajātaka*. Now, if we talk about the Alumni of Odantapuri, the only one that has been found out is Acharya Shri Ganga of Vikramshila, who was an alumnus of Odantapuri and taught at Vikramshila.[36][37]

DESTRUCTION

By the 11th century CE, just like Nalanda, Odantapuri also started facing a decline as only fifty students and some professors were left out of the 12,000 students and 160 professors. In the 12th century AD, as I mentioned in pg. 34 Bakhtiyar Khalji not only destroyed Nalanda but also Vikramshila as well as Odantapuri. It is said that Khalji and his army mistook the monastery as a fortress.[43] In Tabaqat-i-Nasiri, an elaborate history of the Islamic world written in Persian by Minhaj-i Siraj Juzjani, it is described about Odantapuri's tragic end that his army had seized great plunder, killing all the people, mostly were head shaven monks whom they misunderstood as head shaven Brahmins. The army found a large number of books, they wanted someone to explain the content, but nobody was alive to do so. It was then that it was discovered that the entire fort was a place of learning.[42] However, Nalanda and Odantapuri were just a few kilometres away from each other and they both felt the same fate from the same person.[40] Taranatha writes that the ruler of Magadha had fortified Odantapuri and put some soldiers there with whom the monks joined in repulsing the invaders. He also mentioned that one of the early raids in Odantapuri by the Turkic force was driven back.[44]   As per the biography of Dharmasvamin, a Tibetan monk and pilgrim who had visited India between 1234 and 1236 AD, Odantapuri was turned into a military headquarters of the Turkic forces after its destruction.[41] And as the time passed, unfortunately, the Sam-Ye monastery also became ruins.

VIKRAMSHILA

Central Stupa of Vikramshila today   Courtesy: Bihar Tourism

ESTABLISHMENT

There were several Buddhist Viharas and Mahaviharas built during the Pala period in ancient Bengal and Magadha, especially under the rule of Gopala and Dharmapala. Just like Gopala built the Odantapuri, his son and successor Dharmapala constructed and founded the Vikramshila, which served as an extreme rival of Nalanda. Vikramshila was built to become a new Nalanda since the scholarship qualities of Nalanda were declining. However, Vikramshila and Nalanda soon collaborated and the same board managed the affairs of both Nalanda and Vikramshila. Teachers were exchanged between the universities.[1]   Later on, Vikramshila emerged as a great competitor to Nalanda and gained more than 1000 students and 100 teachers. A wide range of subjects were taught at Vikramshila such as philosophy, grammar, metaphysics, Indian logic, etc. which was the main reason for becoming a rival to Nalanda. This Vishwavidyalaya served from the early 9th century AD till the 12th century AD, which means nearly 400 years. It is said that some students of Vikramshila practically formed the culture and civilisation of Tibet.[1]

HIERARCHY

Mr. Sukumar Dutt in his book, Buddhist Monks and Monasteries of India, mentions a more precise hierarchy at Vikramshila than any other Mahaviharas. The top in the list of the hierarchy was the *Adhyakṣa* or abbot, who was the head of the establishment. After him comes the *Dvārapāla*, also known as *Dvārapaṇ ḍ ita*, and the six gate protectors or the gate scholars. Then comes the *Mahapaṇḍita* or great scholars, and then the *Paṇḍita*, or scholars which were roughly 108 in number. Then comes the *Upādhyāya* or *Āchārya*, who were the teachers or professors. Then finally at the end of the list, comes the *bhikṣu*, or the resident monks. In this whole list, the *Adhyakṣa* and the *Dvārapāla* were the most important, since the *Adhyakṣa* were the head of the establishment, but why the *Dvārapāla*? Because they were scholars of high eminence and celebrity. It was also a key post in the leadership of the Vishwavidyalaya, and they were also responsible for conducting the entrance examination of Vikramshila. Taranatha in his writings mentions about such six gatekeepers in Vikramshila during the rule of Chanaka. These six gatekeepers were: Ratnākaraśānti (Eastern Gate), Vāgīsvarakīrti (Western Gate), Ratnavajra (First Central Gate), Jñanasrimitra (Second Central Gate), Naropa (Northern Gate), and Prajñākaramati (Southern Gate). They all were regarded as eminent scholars who had famous works and treatises in their name. One interesting fact is about the ruler Chanaka, who is not known in the Pala history, and according to Taranatha, he is not counted among the seven Palas despite his great services, because he was not from the Pala family. If we talk about the Adhyakṣ a or abbots, the most famous Adhyakṣ a of Vikramshila is Atisa, whom I have mentioned earlier as one of the seventeen great scholars of Nalanda since he was a scholar from Nalanda.[41]

INFRASTRUCTURE

As per one of the evocative inscriptions found at Vikramshila, the wall of the Vishwavidyalaya was decorated with art, and at the right side of the entrance there was a portrait of Nagarjuna, while on the left side was the portrait of Atisha. Inside the university also, there were several portraits of famous scholars and Paṇḍita. Besides this, there were six universities and a central hall in the Vikramshila campus.[1][7][45] The buildings in the campus of Vikramshila were well planned and accommodative. Along with the six universities, there were one hundred and eight temples which were spread out like Lotus Petals. At the centre of the Campus was the beautiful Mahabodhi temple which had six gates leading to the six universities. This central Stupa is still visible in the ruins of Vikramshila today and is probably built on the remains of the Buddha. There also existed a huge residential block meant for the resident monks which was supported by huge pillars, which are now turned into ruins, and the pillars are scattered. Just like Nalanda and Odantapuri, Vikramshila also had a huge library complex where priceless manuscripts were preserved.[46] But unfortunately, most of the manuscripts contained within Vikramshila's library have been lost. So far, only five manuscripts have been identified that contain references to Vikramshila, one of them is currently held at the British Library.[48]

DESTRUCTION

Just like Nalanda and Odantapuri, Vikramshila also became a victim of the attacks of Bakhtiyar Khalji. Not only these three, but Bakhtiyar Khalji and his forces destroyed Somapura, Jagaddala, and Telhara too. He destroyed several major Buddhist monasteries during his raids. As I mentioned earlier, the destruction and decline of Nalanda, Odantapuri, Vikramshila, and other Buddhist Mahaviharas largely contributed to the decline of Buddhism, which already started slowly declining before their destruction. But besides the decline of Buddhism, these destructions also destroyed the tradition of Indian knowledge.[47]

WOMEN EDUCATION IN
VISHWAVIDYALAYA

In ancient India, especially in the Vedic period, women's education was as important as education for men.[1] The general position of women in ancient India was unique. They enjoyed high status and independence in society. Women in ancient India had free access to education. The women not only enjoyed privileged positions but also possessed high standards of morality.[50][51] Saraswati is regarded as the goddess of learning, music, speech, and eloquence, not just in India but wherever the Indian culture left its impression or imprint in Japan, Thailand, Myanmar, Indonesia, and Cambodia.[1] The women in ancient India were expected to participate in Vedic sacrifices and utter mantras. The Rigveda mentions female education and even some of the hymns of the Rigveda have been composed by poetesses such as Visvavara, Lopamudra, Apala, Urvasi, Ghosa, Sulabha, Lilabati, Maitreyi, Saswati, Kshana, Gargi and others.[1][50][51][53] The Upanayana ceremony or the Vedic initiation ceremony was conducted for women too. They positively contributed to the education system.[1][51] Mr. A.S. Altekar in his book, "The

A carving of Goddess Saraswati at Gangaikondacholapuram

Position of Women in Hindu Civilization", mentions the term Upadhyaya which was used to refer to female teachers.[52] There was no Purdah custom in Hindu society before the 12th century, so there was no difficulty for women to choose the teaching profession. The lady teachers may probably have restricted themselves just to the teaching of lady students. There were also special hostels for lady students, which is mentioned by Panini as *Chhatrisala* which would have been probably under the care of lady teachers.[51] During the Vedic period, the age of women at the time of marriage was 16-18 since child or early marriages were not at all the norm during the Vedic period. However, it was in the Mauryan period, that the age of women is said to have fallen to 14-15 at the time of marriage.[1][52] After the Buddha founded the Buddhist Sanghas, he allowed the women to join the Sanghas too. The first female to join the Sangha was the Buddha's maternal aunt Mahaprajapati Gautami. Khema, another woman who joined the Buddhist Sangha, was one of the queens of King Bimbisara. She is considered the first of the Buddha's two chief female disciples, along with Uppalavanna.[54] Even at Nalanda, the females were admitted and given special accommodation. According to both Xuangzang and Yi-Jing, even though there were several men and women in the Vishwavidyalaya, belonging to different nations, there was not a single case of misbehaviour or breach of rules and regulations, which shows the high moral fibre of the students who studied at Nalanda.[49]

One of the best example of a great lady scholar of ancient India was Gargi Vachaknavi of the 7th Century BCE who is also regarded as one of the earliest symbols of Feminism in the world.[55][56] She was the daughter of sage Vachaknu in the lineage of sage Garga. In Vedic literature, she was honoured as a great natural philosopher and expounder of the Vedas. She was one of the great *Brahmavadini*. She was also one of the poetesses who composed hymns in the Rigveda.[1][50]

It is to noted that *Brahmavadini* were the women with the highest philosophical knowledge of Brahman or universal consciousness.[56][57]

An illustration of the debate between Gargi and Yajnavalkya at the court of king Janaka

At a very young age, she became highly knowledgeable in the Vedas and Upanishads and held intellectual debates with other philosophers. In the *Brihadaranyaka Upanishad*, there is an instance of an interesting debate between Gargi and Yajnavalkya, a renowned Vedic sage in the court of King Janaka of Videha kingdom, who is known as the father goddess Sita. In the court of King Janaka, Gargi was the only one to ask questions to Yajnavalkya twice. She challenged Yajnavalkya with such persistent questions on the Brahman involving a subtle understanding of the Shastras, that after answering a few questions, Yajnavalkya declines to take any more interrogation, and then Gargi effectively tells the men to shut up.[1][55]

The interest of learning and transmitting the knowledge preserved in the Vedas and Upanishads in both men and women was the reason why the education system of ancient India was so well developed. Ancient India also witnessed a lot of queens and princesses taking a keen interest in administration of their kingdoms since their education taught them to even fight if necessary.

Rajatarangini by Kalhana describes several queens from Kashmir fighting in the battlefield. Not only them, but the queens of Andhra dynasty and the Vakataka dynasty such as Nayanika and Prabhavatigupta took active part in governance which could not have been possible without female education.[45]

However, from the 12th century onwards, when the Islamic invaders began to control different parts of India, the status of Indian women became low since they were enslaved and sold in the slave market. In the northwest regions of India, especially in the Hindu Rajput kingdoms, practices such as Jauhar became common, where women jumped into fire rather than allow themselves to be humiliated and dishonoured by the invaders. The society was in a great state of disturbance and certainty.

The Indian women became the easiest targets for forced humiliation in all the communities. In this type of situation, the natural tendency is for male members in families to protect the female members. Security took importance over anything else. During the Islamic rule, the social status of women deteriorated and female education declined drastically and the age of marriage reduced too. This was the time when the Purdah system took place and the styles of dressing of Hindu women became more conservative in order to protect them from oppressors.[1][52]

By the time the British rule began in India, except Kerala, where female education was still alive, women were home-bound and received limited or no education.

Thanks to social reformers such as Savitribai and Jyotirao Phule and Ishwar Chandra Vidyasagar who worked zealously for women's education. In Maharashtra, after facing several odds, the Phules successfully started the first ever modern girls school for lower caste girls. While in Bengal, through the efforts of Vidyasagar, institutions like Hindu Balika Vidyalaya managed to make inroads into Hindu middle-class families.

After independence, India put many policies to ensure that education was accessible to all. After the recommendations regarding women's education were made by the University Education Commission (1948 - 1949) The National committee on women's education chaired by Durgabai Deshmukh was set up which comprehensively examined issues regarding the topic in 1958. Over time, a lot of policies and schemes were implemented to ensure that girls and women get to avail every opportunity to gain primary, secondary and advanced education.[1][58][59]

REDISCOVERY OF VISHWAVIDYALAYA

Today, we know about these Vishwavidyalayas of ancient India because of their rediscovery and the discovered facts have been provided to you through this book as the main theme. But some Universities are there, which we know without their rediscovery; one of them I have mentioned in this book. So first of all, let's start with the:

REDISCOVERY OF TAKSHASHILA

Photograph of the excavations of Sirkap, Taxila   Courtesy: Oriental Museum

In 1861, the Archaeological Survey of India, simply known as ASI was founded and it might not be wrong to say that the excavations of Takshashila in 1863-64 was one of the first excavations done by ASI. However, after the death of Sir Alexander Cunningham, the excavations were continued by Sir John Hubert Marshall, who over 21 years between 1913 and 1932 completely exposed the ancient site of Takshashila and its monuments. The whole excavation was filmed and photographed; even today you can find the images of those excavations. John Marshall also wrote a book series named Taxila where he documented the history and topographical background of Takshashila and everything that was found in the excavations at the site.[60]

REDISCOVERY OF NALANDA

Excavation of Nalanda   Courtesy: Google Arts & Culture

In the 1910s, the first-ever excavation at the site of Nalanda was started after the local people told a British Officer about some idols buried in the garden, and then the British Officer passed this information to ASI. The excavation continued for 22 years between 1915 and 1937. However, the excavations were stopped and once again the excavations started 23 years after the Independence of India, and this excavation was led for 8 years between 1974 and 1982.[8][61]   The whole excavation revealed extensive remains of six major brick temples and eleven monasteries arranged on a systematic layout and spread over an area of more than a square kilometre. Besides them, a lot of artefacts and inscriptions were also found which contributed a lot to the research of Nalanda.[61] However, the original campus of the ancient Nalanda Vishwavidyalaya is said to have 16 sq km or 3953 acres but only 1.5 sq km or 370 acres has been excavated so far as per the ASI.[62] In 2006, the former president of India Dr. A.P.J. Abdul Kalam visited the site of Nalanda, and in March of the same year, while addressing a joint session of Bihar State Legislative Assembly proposed the revival of Nalanda Vishwavidyalaya. Agreeing with this idea, a lot of countries such as Singapore, the Philippines, Thailand, China, and many more joined hands together and collaborated for the re-establishment of Nalanda. The Parliament of India passed the Nalanda University Act, 2010 and in September 2014, the first batch of students were enrolled. The State Government of Bihar was quick to allocate 455 acres of land for the University campus at a significant location. This marked the establishment of Nalanda University, and the infrastructural constructions were done in the new campus from 2017 to 2023. The celebrated architect Padma Vibhushan awardee late Ar. B.V. Doshi designed the eco-friendly architecture reflecting the Vaastu of the ancient Nalanda while integrating all modern amenities that match world standards. It is a large carbon footprint-free Net-zero campus, sprawling over acres of greens and 100 acres of water-bodies, truly an abode for learning.[63] Currently, the university boasts over 1000 students, out of which around 270 students belong to foreign countries such as Bhutan, Nepal, USA, Zimbabwe, Myanmar, Argentina, Indonesia, Sri Lanka, and many more![64]

REDISCOVERY OF VIKRAMSHILA

The excavations to find Vikramshila were conducted after the independence of India, which was first conducted by B.P. Sinha of Patna University from 1960 to 1969 and subsequently by ASI from 1972 to 1982.[65] But from February 2024, the excavations at Vikramshila have once again been started by the ASI. This excavation may unearth some more buildings in the Vikramshila campus.[66] Just like Nalanda, The Government of India had also planned a revival for Vikramshila as well, and a package of 500 crore was allocated for it. The Government of Bihar had to provide around 500 acres of land which is yet to be finalised.[67][68] But once the land is finalised and the construction starts, India will once again witness another Vikramshila just like another Nalanda.

REDISCOVERY ATTEMPTS OF ODANTAPURI

Of all the Vishwavidyalayas or universities that I mentioned in my book, a few of them have not been found yet, and one of them is Odantapuri. Despite several efforts, the Archaeologists have not been able to identify the exact location of Odantapuri. According to the accounts of Dharmaswamin (who stayed in Nalanda from 1234 - 1236), Odantapuri was near Nalanda. Unfortunately, there is no physical evidence for this and the distances and directions have not been mentioned clearly. However, according to some scholars, the location of Odantapuri might be today's Bihar Sharif. One major reason for that is according to Tabakat-I-Nasiri, Khalji's troop mistook a Vihara, most probably Odantapuri, for a fort. Bihar Sharif did have a fort, parts of which were visible until the mid-20th century, but the subsequent urbanisation has left no trace of this fort on the ground. Besides these, some Buddhist and Hindu carvings have also been discovered from Bihar Sharif which matches the inscription and accounts of the artefacts associated with Odantapuri. But it's important to note that none of those artefacts were found in their original location, and since they are not very heavy or large they could be easily transported to Bihar Sharif from their original position. With this, very limited Archaeological explorations have been conducted in Bihar Sharif thus far.[69]

CONCLUSION

The Vishwavidyalayas of ancient India serve as a huge testament to the ancient Indian education system. I hope this book will let you understand why these Vishwavidyalayas were a major reason of ancient India being called by the name Sone Ki Chidiya (golden bird). Unfortunately, we cannot get the same education system today because of the modernisation and the change of the people's mindset. A big reason for that is the mental colonisation by the British. Though the physical colonisation by the British ended in 1947, the mental colonisation persists through several socio-economic and cultural mechanisms. But it's not just their fault, but also the kings of ancient India. Had they learned from the destruction of the library of Alexandria, ancient Egypt, the House Of Wisdom of Iraq, and Celsus, then India would have boasted the oldest universities of the world. But it feels good to see the revival of these Vishwavidyalayas happening in India just like Nalanda and the upcoming revival of Vikramshila. We shall keep the legacy of these Vishwavidyalayas alive. We shall let the future generations know that there was a time when India had universities equivalent to today's world class institutes which produced a lot of great scholars.

BIBLIOGRAPHY

1. **Singh, Sahana**. The Educational Heritage of Ancient India: How An Ecosystem Of Learning Was Laid To Waste. s.l. : Notionpress.com, 2017.

2. **Sopam, Reena**. Excavation at ancient Buddhist university site in Bihar's Telhara set to resume. Hindustan Times. [Online] February 03, 2021. https://www.hindustantimes.com/india-news/excavation-at-ancient-buddhist-university-site-in-bihar-s-telhara-set-to-resume-101612327729438.html

3. **B.S. Yadav, Manmohan**. Ancient Indian leaps into Mathematics. s.l. : Birkhauser, 2011.

4. **Majumdar, R.C.** Ancient India. s.l. : Motilal Banarsidass publishing house, 1952.

5. **Shah, N.C.** Origin of Sanskrit, Ayurveda and other Sciences in University of Taxila by Aryans. s.l: Annals of Ayurvedic Medicine, 2018, Vol. 7.

6. **Siddiqui, K.S.** University of Takshashila: An ancient seat of learning. Journal of Social sciences and humanities. [Online]

June 30, 2012.
https://jsshuok.com/oj/index.php/jssh/article/view/233

7. **Mookerji, Radha Kumud.** Ancient Indian education - Brahminical and Buddhist. s.l: Motilal Banarsidass publishing house, 1960.

8. **Kumar, Sanjay.** Archaeological Site of Nalanda Mahavihara (Nalanda University) Gets Inscribed in World Heritage List. Press Information Bureau
Government of India, Ministry of Culture. [Online] July 5, 2016.
https://pib.gov.in/newsite/PrintRelease.aspx?relid=147142#:~:text=Nalanda%20Mahavihara%20was%20founded%20by,as%20well%20as%20various%20scholars.

9. **BSTDC**, Bihar State Tourism Development Corporation. Nalanda. Government of Bihar. [Online]
https://bstdc.bihar.gov.in/nalanda.htm

10. **R, Yashaswini**. Nalanda University. Infinity: An official educational blog for BCsians. [Online] April 15, 2020.
https://infinity.bgscollege.in/post/nalanda-university#:~:text=It%20was%20the%20Guptas%20in,a%20structure%20within%20the%20campus.

11. **Dube, Sanjiv.** Nalanda varsity ruins in Unesco heritage list. Academics-India.com. [Online] http://www.academics-india.com/nalanda.htm#:~:text=As%20per%20ASI%20record s%2C%20subjects,1%20sq%20km%20is%20excavated.

12. **Singh, Sahana.** Revisiting The Educational Heritage of India. s.l. : Vitasta Publishing pvt ltd, 2022.

13. **Ring, Trudy.** International Dictionary of Historic Places: Asia and Oceania.
Volume 5 of International Dictionary of Historic Places. s.l. : Taylor & Francis, 1994.

14. **Frazier, Jessica; Flood, Gavin.** The Continuum Companion to Hindu Studies. Bloomsbury Companions. Continuum Companions Series. s.l. : A&C Black, 2011.

15. **Berzin, Dr. Alexander.** The Four Buddhist Tenet Systems Regarding Illusion. The Indian Tenet Systems. [Online] https://web.archive.org/web/20160815193010/http://studybud dhism.com/en/advanced-studies/abhidharma-tenet-systems/the-indian-tenet-systems/the-four-buddhist-tenet-systems-regarding-illusion

16. The Nalanda Criteria. Tribune India. [Online] 23 July, 2016. https://www.tribuneindia.com/news/archive/comment/the-nalanda-criteria-269685

17. **Mukherjee, Sugato.** Nalanda: The university that changed the world. BBC. [Online] February 24, 2023. https://www.bbc.com/travel/article/20230222-nalanda-the-university-that-changed-the-world

18. Seventeen Great Scholars of Nalanda Monastery. Himalayan Art Resources. [Online] https://www.himalayanart.org/search/set.cfm?setID=2533

19. The Seventeen Pandits of Nalanda Monastery. Nalanda masters. Fpmt. [Online] July-September 2012. https://fpmt.org/mandala/archives/mandala-for-2012/july/the-seventeen-pandits-of-nalanda-monastery/July-September, 2012. https://fpmt.org/mandala/archives/mandala-for-2012/july/the-seventeen-pandits-of-nalanda-monastery/

20. **Garfield, Jay L.** The Fundamental Wisdom of the Middle Way. s.l. : Oxford: Oxford University Press, 1995.

21. **Wei Hong, Zheng.** Dignāga and Dharmakīrti: Two Summits of Indian Buddhist Logic. Shanghai, China, Research Institute of Chinese Classics; Fudan University, n.d.

22. **Jarzombek, Mark M.; Prakash, Vikramaditya; Ching, Francis D.K.** A Global History of Architecture. s.l. : Wiley, 2011.

23. Nalanda. Government of Bihar. [Online] n.d. : https://nalanda.nic.in/en/tourist-place/ancient-nalanda-universitys-ruins/

24. **Sankalia, H.D.** The University of Nalanda. s.l. : B.G. Paul and Co. Publishers, 1934.

25. **Dey, Dr. Amit.** Aspects of Bhakti movement in India. University of Calcutta. [Online] n.d. : https://www.caluniv.ac.in/academic/History/Study/Bhakti-Saint.pdf

26. **Leigh-Howarth, Jake.** The Sena Empire: Rise and Fall of the Last Hindu Kings of Bengal. Ancient Origins. [Online] 2 May 2022. https://www.ancient-origins.net/history-famous-people/sena-empire-0016707

27. **Majumdar, R.C.** The history of Bengal. s.l. : University of Dacca, 1943.

28. **Patil, D.R.** Antiquarian remains in Bihar. s.l. : K.P. Jaiswal research institute, 1963.

29. **Tyagi, Satish Kumar, Jha, Tushar Kant.** Contours Of The Political Legitimation Strategy Of The Rulers Of Pala Dynasty In Bengal- Bihar (CE 730 TO CE 1165). Proceedings

of the Indian History Congress. s.l. : Indian History Congress, 2016.

30. **Dahiya, Poonam Dalal.** Ancient And Medieval India. s.l. : McGraw-Hill Education, 2017

31. **Balogh, Daniel.** Pithipati Puzzles: Custodians of the Diamond Throne. s.l. : British Museum Research Publications, 2021.

32. **Majumdar, R.C.** The History and Culture of the Indian People. s.l. : Bharatiya Vidya Bhavan, 1964.

33. **Bose, Mainak Kumar.** Late Classical India. s.l. : A. Mukherjee & Company, 1988.

34. **Taranatha, Jo Nang.** The Seven Instruction Lineages. s.l. : Library of Tibetan Works and Archives, 2007.

35. **Powers, John.** Introduction to Tibetan Buddhism. s.l. : Shambhala publications, 2007.

36. **Barua, Karan Baran.** Odantapuri Mahavihara. Research Gate. [Online] August 2018. https://www.researchgate.net/publication/326982087_Odantap uri_Mahavihara_India

37. Odantapuri. IndiaNetZone. [Online] n.d. https://www.indianetzone.com/76/odantapuri.htm

38. **Shrimali, Krishna Mohan.** Buddhism Under The Palas— A Study Based On Taranatha. Proceedings of Indian History Congress. s.l. : Indian History Congress, 1970.

39. **Ston, Bu, E., Obermiller.** History of Buddhism; part 2 History of Buddhism in India Tibet. s.l. : Heidelberg, 1932.

40. **Ghosh, Amalandala.** A Guide to Nalanda. New Delhi: The Archaeological Survey of India, 1965.

41. **Dutt, Sukumar.** Buddhist Monks and Monasteries of India: Their History and Their Contribution to Indian Culture. s.l. : Motilal Banarsidass publishing house, 1988.

42. **Minhaj-Ud-Din, Maulana.** Tabakat-I-Nasiri: A General History Of The Muhammadan Dynasties Of Asia Including Hindustan. s.l. : Cilbert & Rivington, 1881.

43. **Rajani, M.B, Kumar, V.** Where Was Odantapuri Located?. Reson 26, 1287–1304. [Online] 30 October, 2021. https://doi.org/10.1007/s12045-021-1230-0

44. **Singh, Anand.** Destruction' and 'Decline' of Nālandā Mahāvihāra: Prejudices and Praxis. Journal of the Royal Asiatic

Society of Sri Lanka. s.l. : Royal Asiatic Society of Sri Lanka (RASSL)

45. **Altekar A.S.** Education in Ancient India. s.l. : NandKishore and Bros, 1944.

46. **Hussain, M.D. Neyaz.** The Ancient University of Vikramshila (Part - 1). Pg History Sem - 2 Paper Cc:7. S.L. : Pg Department Of History, Maharaja College, Vksu, Ara (Bihar), n.d.

47. **BSTDC,** Bihar State Tourism Development Corporation. Vikramshila. Government of Bihar. [Online] n.d. https://bstdc.bihar.gov.in/vikramshila.htm

48. **Delhey, Martin.** The Library at the East Indian Buddhist Monastery of Vikramaśīla: an Attempt to Identify Its Himalayan Remains. s.l. : Centre for the Study of Manuscript Cultures: 2–26, 2016.

49. **Murthy, B.M.N.** The glory of Nalanda. One India One People. [Online] 1 March, 2014. https://oneindiaonepeople.com/the-glory-of-nalanda/

50. **Sharma, Twinkle.** Women's Education in Ancient India. Central Asian Journal of Social Sciences and History. [Online] 30 August, 2020.

https://cajssh.centralasianstudies.org/index.php/CAJSSH/articl e/view/39

51. **Kashyap, Diksha.** Women's Education in Ancient India. Your Article Library. [Online] n.d. https://www.yourarticlelibrary.com/education/womens-education/womens-education-in-ancient-india/63492

52. **Altekar, A.S.** The Position of Women in Hindu Civilization: from Prehistoric Times to the Present Day. Delhi: Motilal Banarsidass Publications, 1938.

53. **Sharma, Anita.** Women In Ancient India: Education And Empowerment. International Journal of Innovations & Research Analysis (IJIRA). [Online] January, 2023. https://inspirajournals.com/uploads/Issues/883493537.pdf

54. **Emmanuel, Steven M.** A Companion to Buddhist Philosophy. s.l. : John Wiley & Sons, 22 Jan 2013

55. **Olivelle, Patrick.** Gargi Vachaknavi – India's first woman philosopher who 'shut up' men in King Janaka's court. The Print. [Online] 03 January, 2024 https://theprint.in/opinion/theprint-purana/gargi-vachaknavi-indias-first-woman-philosopher-who-shut-up-men-in-king-janakas-court/1908896/

56. Devvrat Yoga. Gargi Vachaknavi. Devvrat Yoga Kerala. [Online] n.d. https://www.devvratyoga.com/gargi-vachaknavi/#:~:text=The%20great%20Indian%20sage%20Ga rgi,renowned%20exponent%20of%20Vedic%20literature.

57. **Banerji, Sures Chandra.** A Companion to Sanskrit Literature: Spanning a Period of Over Three Thousand Years, Containing Brief Accounts of Authors, Works, Characters, Technical Terms, Geographical Names, Myths, Legends and Several Appendices. s.l. : Motilal Banarsidass Publications, 1989.

58. **Roy, Sanghamitra Basu.** An Analysis Of Ishwar Chandra Vidyasagar As Pioneer Of Woman Education. International Journal of Advanced Research. [Online] January 2022. https://www.researchgate.net/publication/358373012_AN_AN ALYSIS_OF_ISHWAR_CHANDRA_VIDYASAGAR_AS_P IONEER_OF_WOMAN_EDUCATION

59. **Goswami, Ruchika.** Explained: The legacy of Savitribai and Jyotirao Phule. The Indian Express. [Online] 8 March, 2022. https://indianexpress.com/article/explained/explained-who-are-the-phules-what-is-the-row-around-maharashtra-governors-remarks-on-them-7805497/

60. Taxila in Focus. Oriental Museum, Durham University. [Online] n.d.

https://stories.durham.ac.uk/TaxilaInFocus/#:~:text=Marshall%20began%20a%20sustained%2021,20th%20century%20South%20Asia.

61. Excavated Site, Nalanda Ticketed Monuments. Ek Bharat Shreshtha Bharat. [Online] n.d. https://ekbharat.gov.in/Document/DigitalResources/20.Excavated%20Site,%20Nalanda.pdf

62. **Bhuvan.** Cartosat-1 views the Nalanda Buddhist ruins - Bhuvan. Indian Geo Platform of ISRO. [Online] n.d. https://bhuvan-app1.nrsc.gov.in/tourism/documents/nalanda_nrsc.pdf

63. History and Revival. Nalanda University. [Online] n.d. https://nalandauniv.edu.in/about-nalanda/history-and-revival/

64. International community. Nalanda University. [Online] n.d. https://nalandauniv.edu.in/international-community/#:~:text=For%20the%20academic%20year%202020 22,had%20822%20students%20in%20total.

65. **Chaudhary, Pranava K.** ASI to develop the ancient site of Vikramshila Mahavihara. Times Of India. [Online] 10 October, 2009. https://timesofindia.indiatimes.com/city/patna/ASI-to-develop-ancient-site-of-Vikramshila-Mahavihara/articleshow/5107966.cms

66. **PTI.** ASI starts excavation to further unearth remnants of Vikramasila Mahavihara. Deccan Herald. [Online] 18 February, 2024. https://www.deccanherald.com/india/bihar/asi-starts-excavation-to-further-unearth-remnants-of-vikramasila-mahavihara-2899648

67. **Anand, Abhay.** PM Modi's dream to revive ancient Vikramshila University still a distant dream. Shiksha. [Online] 11 August, 2021. https://www.shiksha.com/news/humanities-social-sciences-pm-modi-s-dream-to-revive-ancient-vikramshila-university-still-a-distant-dream-blogId-66099

68. **PTI.** Pranab hopeful of reviving Vikramshila University. The Hindu. [Online] 03 April, 2017. https://www.thehindu.com/news/national/other-states/pranab-hopeful-of-reviving-vikramshila-university/article17780837.ece

69. Where Was Odantapuri Located?* Archaeological Evidence ... . Indian Academy of Sciences. [Online] 9 January, 2014. https://www.ias.ac.in/public/Volumes/reso/026/09/1287-1304.pdf

ABOUT THE AUTHOR

Anurodh Das is an aspiring young historian and writer with a deep passion for uncovering and sharing hidden historical narratives. Despite being only 14 years old, he has authored numerous articles on historical and cultural topics, which have been published on platforms such as LinkedIn, Voices Of Youth - UNICEF, MDPI Encyclopedia, Youth Ki Awaaz, and World History Encyclopedia. Anurodh writes with the aim of invoking wider interest in history and culture, particularly among the youth.

In addition to his writing, Anurodh is actively involved in content creation. He runs a YouTube channel named "RODH's ZONE," where he shares content related to history, animations, and current affairs. His channel has garnered a growing community of 1.4k subscribers. Furthermore, Anurodh has penned a historical drama screenplay titled "NAWAB-ZADA: A Prince's Chronicles," which he submitted to the Atlanta Film Festival Screenplay Writing Competition 2024. His dedication to historical inquiry and education is evident in all his creative and scholarly pursuits.